Country ABCs

The
United States
ABCs

A Book About the People and Places
of the United States of America

Written by Holly Schroeder • Illustrated by Jeff Yesh

Special thanks to our advisers for their expertise:
Paul R. Baker, Ph.D.
Professor of History, Emeritus
New York University, New York City

Susan Kesselring, M.A., Literacy Educator
Rosemount-Apple Valley-Eagan (Minnesota) School District

PICTURE WINDOW BOOKS
Minneapolis, Minnesota

Managing Editor: Bob Temple
Creative Director: Terri Foley
Editor: Nadia Higgins
Editorial Adviser: Andrea Cascardi
Copy Editor: Laurie Kahn
Designer: John Moldstad
Page production: Picture Window Books
The illustrations in this book were prepared digitally.

Picture Window Books
5115 Excelsior Boulevard
Suite 232
Minneapolis, MN 55416
1-877-845-8392
www.picturewindowbooks.com

Printed in the United States of America.

Library of Congress Cataloging-in-Publication Data
Schroeder, Holly.
The United States ABCs : a book about the people and places of the United States /
written by Holly Schroeder ; illustrated by Jeff Yesh.
p. cm. — (Country ABCs)
Summary: An alphabetical exploration of the people, geography,
animals, plants, history, and culture of the United States.
Includes bibliographical references and index.
ISBN 1-4048-0181-2 (Reinforced Library Binding)
1. United States—Juvenile literature. 2. English language—
Alphabet—Juvenile literature. [1. United States. 2. Alphabet.]
I. Title. II. Series.
E156 .S34 2004
973—dc22
2003016527

Welcome to the United States of America!

The United States is a huge country in North America. It is the richest country in the world. More than 280 million people live in the United States. It is ranked third in world population.

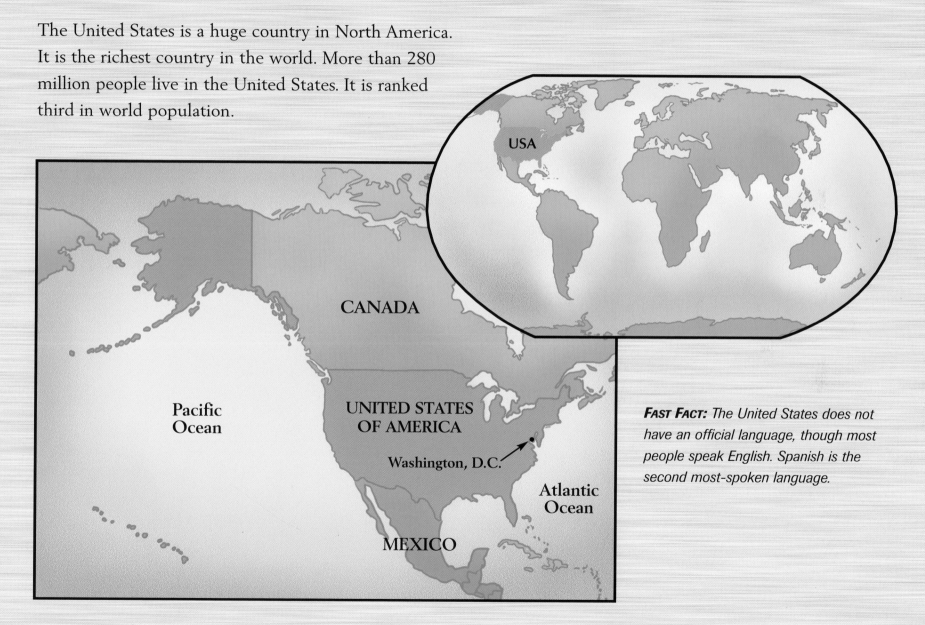

USA

CANADA

Pacific
Ocean

UNITED STATES
OF AMERICA

Washington, D.C.

Atlantic
Ocean

MEXICO

FAST FACT: The United States does not have an official language, though most people speak English. Spanish is the second most-spoken language.

A is for **a**utomobiles.

About 100 years ago, Americans made the first automobiles that could be used in daily life. Today, more cars zip along U.S. roads than in any other country. The United States is also one of the two biggest automobile producers in the world.

This is how cars looked in the early 1900s.

Bb

About 50 million Americans go to major league baseball games every year—and millions more watch the games on TV. Children often start playing baseball even before they go to school. The country's love of baseball is so famous that the sport has been nicknamed The Great American Pastime.

FAST FACT: *People in the United States began playing baseball in the mid-1800s. The first professional team, called the Cincinnati Red Stockings, was formed in 1869.*

C is for Constitution.

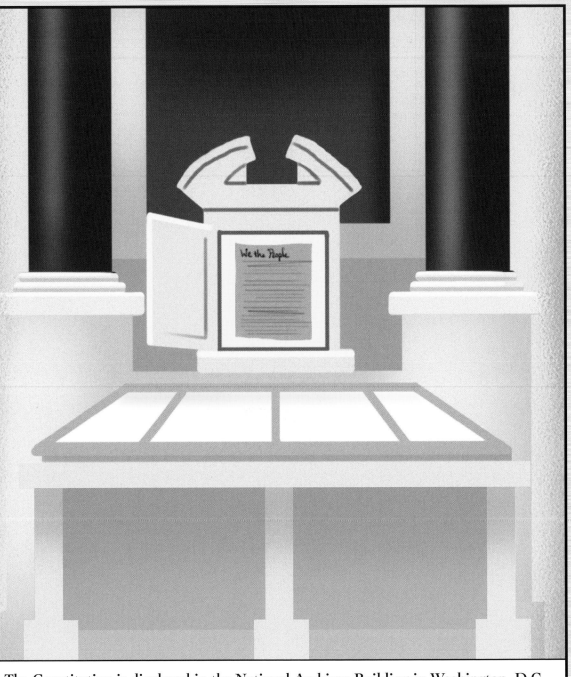

In 1787, the United States had recently won its independence from Great Britain. Now the 13 original states needed to decide what kind of government would rule their new country. Representatives from the states met in Philadelphia. They created the Constitution of the United States. This remarkable document outlines the U.S. government as it is known today.

The Constitution is displayed in the National Archives Building in Washington, D.C.

D is for dollar.

The dollar is the United States's basic unit of money. Dollars come in $1, $2, $5, $10, $20, $50, and $100 bills. A dollar is made up of 100 cents. Common U.S. coins are the penny (one cent), nickel (five cents), dime (10 cents), and quarter (25 cents).

FAST FACT: *For a short time in 1934 and 1935, the U.S. Treasury printed a $100,000 bill. That bill featured a picture of former president Woodrow Wilson.*

E is for eagle.

The bald eagle soars only in the skies of North America. This huge, powerful bird was chosen as the national bird by the country's early leaders. Thirty years ago, the bald eagle was nearly extinct. Since then, the government has worked to protect the eagle. Today, this rare bird is making a comeback.

Ee

F is for farmers.

Ff

American farmers work with some of the richest soil in the world. They use scientific farming methods and huge machines to grow tons of food. Fewer than 2 percent of Americans are farmers, but they grow enough food to feed the whole country—with plenty extra to sell to other countries.

FAST FACT: In the early days of the country, most families lived on small farms.

G is for Grand Canyon.

Six million years ago, the Colorado River began sweeping away tiny bits of the stone that formed its banks. Over time, the river carved out one of the most spectacular landforms in the world—the Grand Canyon. The huge canyon is one mile (1.6 kilometers) deep in some places.

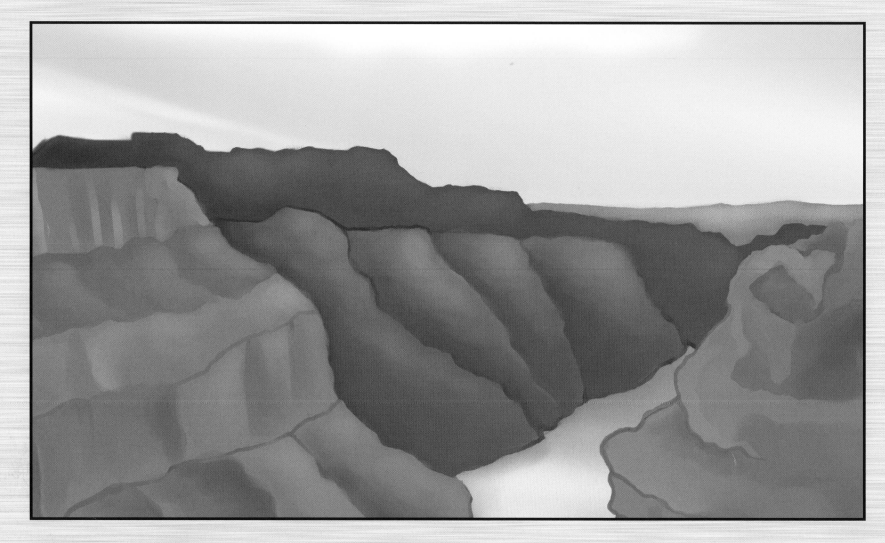

FAST FACT: Hikers can make the difficult walk down the canyon on steep, winding trails. Some people ride mules down and camp overnight on the canyon's floor.

H is for Hollywood.

Hollywood's huge sign stands on a hill in southern California. The sign is a famous landmark of this town, which is considered the movie capital of the world. Each year, millions of tourists come to Hollywood to visit studios where movies are filmed. The tourists stroll down Hollywood's Walk of Fame in hopes of seeing a movie star.

I is for immigrants.

Immigrants are people who have left their homelands to live in other countries. The United States is a nation of immigrants. People from just about every country in the world live here. Many came looking for work in this rich country. Others sought freedom from troubles in their own lands.

This statue, called the Statue of Liberty, stands in New York's harbor.
For many immigrants, it has represented the freedom of their new country.

12

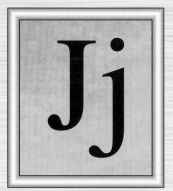

J is for jazz.

Many people say jazz is the only art form that began in the United States. Black musicians in New Orleans, Louisiana, developed jazz about 100 years ago. These musicians would surprise listeners by inventing some of the music as they went along. This part of jazz, called improvisation, is one of the things that make this music so original.

Louis Armstrong was one of the most famous jazz musicians.

K is for Martin Luther King Jr.

"I have a dream." These words mark one of the most famous speeches in American history. Martin Luther King Jr. spoke these words to a huge crowd in Washington, D.C., in 1963. King's dream was that black people and white people could live side by side as equals. King was an important civil rights leader. He was murdered in 1968, but many people are carrying on his dream today.

FAST FACT: King's birthday is a national holiday in the United States. It is celebrated on the third Monday of January.

L is for Abraham Lincoln.

Abraham Lincoln is one of the most admired presidents in American history. He led the country during the Civil War (1861–1865), when the Southern states tried to break away from the United States and become their own country. He also helped free black slaves in the South.

This statue of Abraham Lincoln is 19 feet (5.8 meters) high.
It is part of the Lincoln Memorial in Washington, D.C.

M is for *Mayflower*.

In 1620, 102 English people sailed across the Atlantic Ocean on a ship called the *Mayflower*. They were in search of a new life in the land that was to become the United States. These early settlers, or Pilgrims, landed on the coast of what is now Massachusetts.

FAST FACT: *The first winter in their new land was hard on the settlers. About half of the original 102 died from cold and lack of food.*

N is for Navajo Indians.

Navajo Indians are one of the many nations of American Indians that have been living in North America for thousands of years. As European settlers arrived, they eventually took over almost all of the Indians' land. Today, most Navajo live on their own reservation in the Southwest. It is the country's biggest Indian reservation.

FAST FACT: *Beautiful turquoise jewelry and woven rugs are specialities of Navajo artists.*

O is for outer space.

The U.S. space program began in 1958. It has launched many rockets into outer space. In 1969, Neil Armstrong became the first person to walk on the moon. Unmanned U.S. spacecraft have landed on Mars and circled other planets and asteroids.

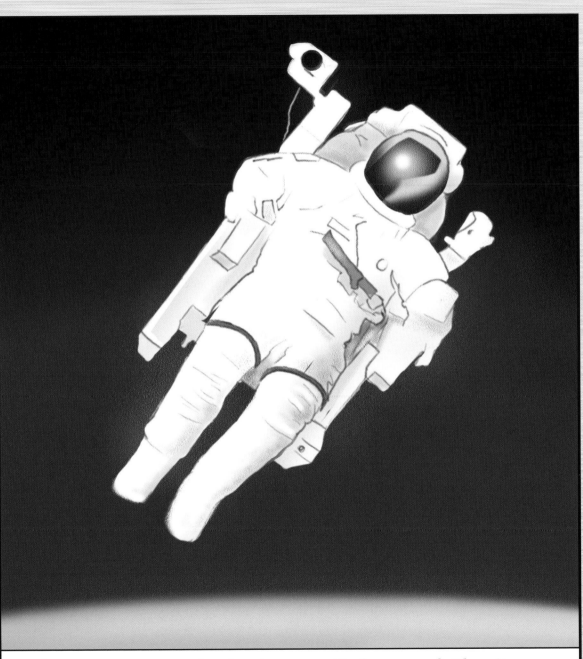

Astronauts wear space suits when they go outside the spacecraft. The suits provide air for breathing. They protect astronauts from the sun's harmful rays.

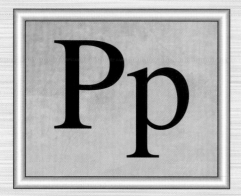

P is for popcorn.

Popcorn, Popsicles, and potato chips are all foods that originated in the United States. Today pizza is an American favorite, too—though pizza originally came from Italy. Like many foods eaten in the United States, pizza was introduced to Americans by immigrants.

FAST FACT: *Popcorn was introduced to Pilgrims by the American Indians and was eaten at the first Thanksgiving.*

Q is for Quakers.

Qq

Quakers came to Colonial America from England in the 1600s. They came seeking freedom to practice their religion. Today, more Quakers live in the United States than in any other country. Throughout American history, Quakers have been known for being against war. Unlike other white settlers, Quakers were quick to make peace with their Indian neighbors.

FAST FACT: *Most Americans are Christian. Muslims belong to Islam, the fastest growing religion in the country.*

Rr

Thick forests of giant redwood trees grow along the coast of California. As high as skyscrapers, the trees are the tallest in the world. Their thick trunks are as wide as cars.

FAST FACT: *The United States has many different kinds of forests. Forests still cover about one-third of the land.*

21

S is for Stars and Stripes.

Stars and Stripes is a nickname for the U.S. flag. The 13 red and white stripes stand for the 13 original colonies. The 50 stars represent the 50 states. The first flag had just 13 stars. The design has changed many times as more states have been added.

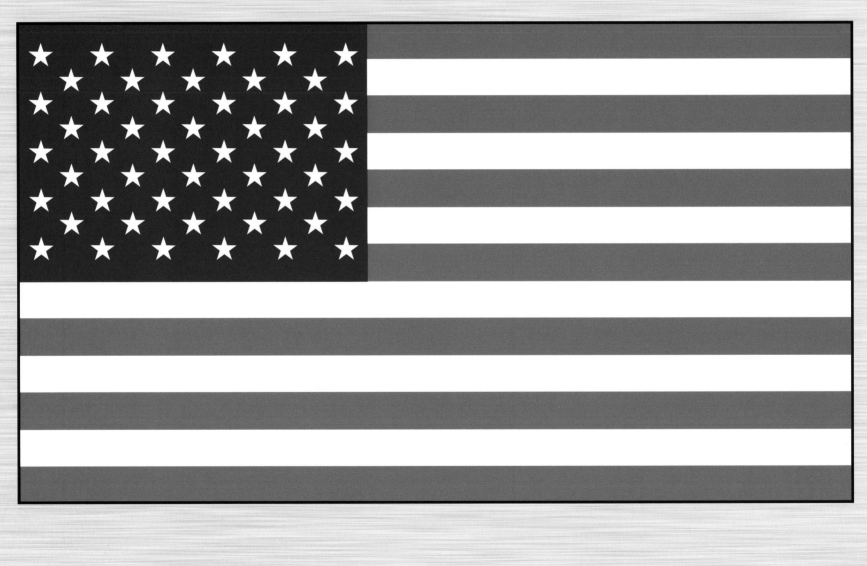

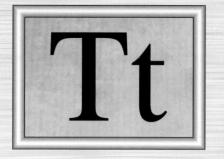

T is for tornadoes.

These dangerous storms look like long, twisting clouds that stretch from the ground into the sky. The United States has more tornadoes than any other country. Most tornadoes last only a few minutes. But in that short time, they can lift cars and houses into the air and destroy entire towns.

FAST FACT: Tornado Alley refers to a region of midwestern and southern states. Most tornadoes happen here, particularly in Texas, Oklahoma, Kansas, Nebraska, and Iowa.

U is for United Nations.

After World War II (1939–1945), the United States and other countries decided that such a horrible war must never happen again. So they started an organization called the United Nations, or UN. Almost every country belongs to the United Nations. Its goal is to bring peace to the world.

This picture shows the United Nations headquarters in New York City. The flags of all the 191 member countries fly outside.

Vv

V is for voting.

On Election Day, Americans vote for the country's leaders. Voters line up outside polling places in their neighborhoods. A polling place can be a school, a church, or even the local fire station. Voters stand in booths where they can make their choices in private.

FAST FACT: *Black men were given the right to vote in 1870.*
Women were not allowed to vote until 1920.

W is for Washington, D.C.

Washington, D.C., is the country's capital. It was named after George Washington, the first U.S. president. In 1791, George Washington chose the city's location in the eastern part of the country, between Maryland and Virginia.

The U.S. president lives in this building, called the White House.
The White House is at 1600 Pennsylvania Avenue in Washington, D.C.

The United States exports, or sells, huge amounts of food to other countries. In fact, it is the biggest food exporter in the world. Car parts, computers, and airplanes are other important exports.

FAST FACT: *The United States is, by far, the richest country in the world. The total value of all its goods and services in one year is twice as much as that of Japan, which is the second richest country.*

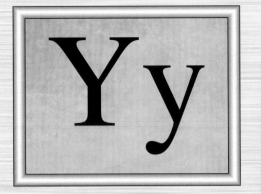

Y is for Yellowstone.

Deep inside the earth under Yellowstone National Park lies a huge pool of melted rock. Water seeps down into this hot spot. The water heats up quickly, then explodes through narrow cracks in the ground. These explosions of water, called geysers, are the park's most famous attraction.

This geyser, called Old Faithful, is at Yellowstone Park. Old Faithful has erupted several times a day for the last several decades.

Z is for zipper.

Zz

The United States is known for its many inventors. The zipper was invented by an American in 1893. Other American inventions include everything from the lightbulb and the Internet to cola and blue jeans.

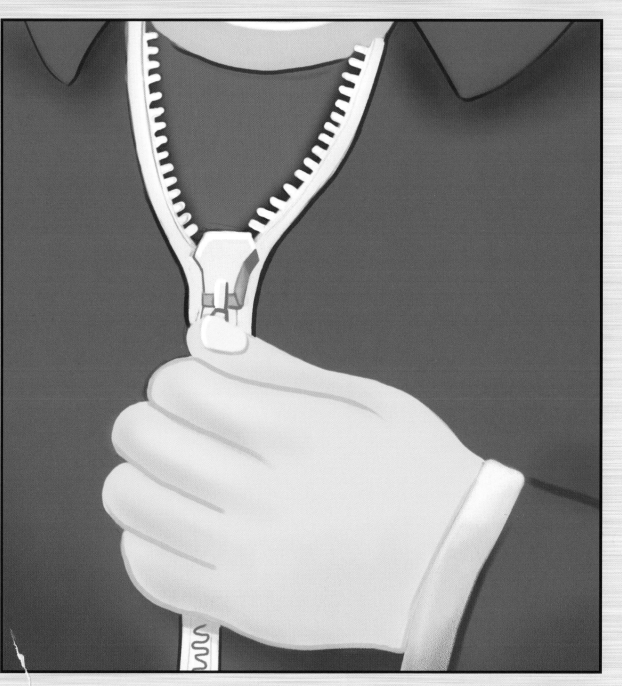

FAST FACT: *The zipper got its name from the sound it makes as it's pulled up and down.*

HIGHWOOD PUBLIC LIBRARY

The United States in Brief

Official Name: United States of America

Capital: Washington, D.C. (572,059 people)

Language: English (Spanish spoken by a large minority)

Population: 280,562,489

People: 75% white; 13% Hispanic (may also be white, black, or American Indian); 12% black; 4% Asian American; 1–2% American Indian and Alaskan and Hawaiian natives

Religion: Most people (84%) are Christian.

Education: free through 12th grade; required until age 16

Major holidays: New Year's Day (January 1); Memorial Day (last Monday in May); Independence Day (July 4); Labor Day (first Monday in September); Thanksgiving (fourth Thursday in November); Christmas (December 25)

Transportation: Automobiles are the most popular form of transportation. There are 55 cars for every 100 Americans.

Climate: varies greatly from region to region; tropical in Hawaii and Florida, arctic in Alaska, and hot and dry in the Southwestern deserts

Area: 3,615,276 square miles (9,363,520 square kilometers)

Highest point: Mount McKinley, Alaska, at 20,321 feet (6,194 meters)

Lowest point: Death Valley, California, at 282 feet (86 meters) below sea level

Type of government: federal republic

Head of government: president

Major industries: petroleum, steel, motor vehicles, aerospace

Natural resources: coal, copper, lead, iron, natural gas

Major agricultural products: wheat, corn, fruits, vegetables, dairy products

Chief exports: automobiles, industrial supplies, agricultural products

Money: United States dollar

English Around the Country

People in different areas of the United States have their own ways of saying certain things. Here's a sampling of words you might hear people say in particular regions.

EAST COAST

bubbler—a water fountain

frappe/cabinet—a milkshake

hero/hoagie/grinder—a submarine sandwich

pie—a pizza

wicked—very or extremely. "My new skateboard is wicked cool!"

MIDWEST

pop—soda

uff da!—oh boy!

you betcha— definitely; you bet

SOUTHEAST

a piece—a short distance. "The store is down the road a piece."

a spell—for a time. "I sat on the porch for a spell."

fixin' to—getting ready. "I'm fixin' to get some lunch."

y'all—all of you (said to a group of people). "Y'all come back and visit us again sometime!"

Glossary

civil rights—freedoms that every person should have. In the '50s and '60s, black Americans still did not have full civil rights. They led a civil rights movement to get the government to give them the rights they deserved.

Muslim—a follower of a religion called Islam

Pilgrims—early English settlers on the land that later became the United States

reservation—an area set aside as a homeland for American Indians and Alaska natives

turquoise—a blue-green gemstone

To Learn More

At the Library

Bates, Katharine Lee. *America the Beautiful.* New York,
Putnam, 2003.

Catrow, David. *We the Kids: The Preamble to the Constitution
of the United States.* New York: Dial Books for
Young Readers, 2002.

Hopkins, Lee Bennett. *Hand in Hand: An American History
Through Poetry.* New York: Simon & Schuster, 1994.

Miller, Millie, and Cyndi Nelson. *The United States of America:
A State-by-State* Guide. New York: Scholastic
Reference, 1999.

On the Web

Fact Hound

Fact Hound offers a safe, fun way to find Web sites related to this book.
All of the sites on Fact Hound have been researched by our staff.
http://www.facthound.com

1. Visit the Fact Hound home page.
2. Enter a search word related to this book,
   or type in this special code: 1404801812.
3. Click on the FETCH IT button.

Your trusty Fact Hound will fetch the best sites for you!

Index

For my two pea pod babies, as different as can be—Jake and Lucy

—K.B.

For Iry and Bobby

—S.W.

Text copyright © 2003 by Karen Baicker
Illustrations copyright © 2003 by Sam Williams
CIP Data is available

"Pea Pod Babies" is a trademark of Karen Baicker and Sam Williams

Published in the United States in 2003 by Handprint Books
413 Sixth Avenue
Brooklyn, New York 11215
www.handprintbooks.com

First Edition
Printed in China
ISBN:1-59354-003-5
2 4 6 8 10 9 7 5 3 1

Pea Pod Babies

Karen Baicker and Sam Williams

HANDPRINT BOOKS 🖐 BROOKLYN, NEW YORK

Once upon a time, a lovely garden bloomed
with rosemary and Queen Anne's lace,
And, of course, a special place
where all the babies grew.

Beyond the bluebells and the beans
hidden deep within the greens,
For those who closely look to see
a magical garden nursery.

And swaying gently in the breeze
there rocked a pod with baby peas.

Tucking them in tenderly
Mama kisses them—
one, two, three.

"Wee baby Sweet Pea,
Sugarplum Snap Pea,
Darling little Snow Pea,
Look at you perfect peas in a pod!"

The neighbor ladies
come to see
those babies in a line,

As cute as cute as cute can be,

Three pea pod babies on the vine.

Mama and all her garden friends
cootchie-coo them to no end.
"One and two and three little nosies,
Count all thirty tiny toesies.
Six plump cheeks, six button eyes
smooshed together honey pies."

"Just like peas in a pod," they say
(at least three dozen times a day).
But anyone can plainly see
that they're as different as can be!

Soon the pea pod babies had had more than enough
of all the ooka-booka-pooka samey-samey stuff.
And then one truly fateful day
the neighbor ladies came to say:

"Peek-a-baby, peek-a-baby, boo, boo, boo!

Look at what we've made for you!

Pat-a-cake, pat-a-cake, pat, pat, pat,

Baby peas in matching hats!

Now how adorable is that?"

Not at all adorable!

Scratchy! Match-y!

Horrible!

Well, Sweet Pea wailed

and Snow Pea pouted.

"No hats, no way!" Snap Pea shouted.

Then they kicked and hopped
'till the pea pod

Popped!

Sweet Pea's Adventure

Scramble down the trellis,

Plop into the lettuce,

Sit up with the buttercup,

Dance around the daisy.

Snow Pea's Adventure

"Here I come! Look at me!"
Snow Pea slides down,
Whoop-dee wheeee!

Throwing his hat down on the ground,

Wearing a cabbage as a crown,

Snap Pea's Adventure

Snap Pea calls, "Look out below!"
And swings from the vine,
"Geronimo!"

Honeysuckle peony
oh-so-happy Sweetie Pea,

Picking a bunch of
wildflowers,
Her hat makes
a beautiful basket,

Daydreamy Sweet Pea strolls along
humming a-tisket, a-tasket.

Roly-poly belly laugh, Snow Pea—what a goofy clown!

Poking about in the dirt for slugs,
Tossing Snow Pea a hatful of bugs.

Sweet Pea's Adventure

Blowing a dandelion puff,
Sweet Pea wishes (and sure enough),
A little stone table is set for three
to visit for a cup of tea.

Snow Pea's Adventure

Just look at that silly tot,
Now Snow Pea's
in the turnip pot.

What does he see?
It's a furry brown bunny.

Snap Pea's Adventure

Stomp a puddle
splishy-splashy,
Oh that muddy
messy Snap Pea!

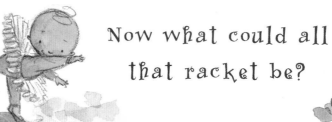

Now what could all
that racket be?

But what was that chirping
and twitting she heard?
The ta-whit-ta-whoo
of a mockingbird,

Calling her
to come along
to see a bit more
of the world.

Hop along after him, Isn't he funny?

It must be
Snap Pea,
naturally!

Clang-a-bang
on the wheelbarrow,
Hop on in
and here we go!

Sweet Pea's Adventure

So Sweet Pea follows
by and by,
Gathering berries
for three-berry pie.

Snow Pea's Adventure

Then Snow Pea hides
from the other guys,

Ready and waiting
to shout SURPRISE!

Snap Pea's Adventure

Rolling into crimson clover
topple eevy-ivy-over.

And skips along
to the garden wall,
Just in time
to see Snap Pea fall!

Here comes Sweet Pea down the path
and Snow Pea tries hard not to laugh,
But suddenly he hears a crash—
It's Snap Pea in the briar patch!

Scrappy Snap Pea scrapes and scrambles
and tumbles into ouchy brambles!
Sweet Pea and Snow Pea race and rush
to help pull Snap Pea from the brush.

Then together happily, they come back to the nursery.

"Pea pod babies! How I missed you!
Come over here and let me kiss you!"

"One, two, three, but I can see...
You don't seem quite the same.

Why, Sweet Pea baby, look at you,
You've made a daisy chain!

Look at that red cherry
stuck on Snow Pea's nose!

Snap Pea, what's that ivy
doing in between your toes?

And what have you done with your matching hats?
Oh, never mind! Just welcome back."

Back into their downy pod,
Rock-a-baby, wink and nod.
Three pea pod babies
but not just-the-samies,
Not as alike as they seem.
Tucked in so tightly,
Sleeping delightly,
Dreaming their own
pea pod dreams.

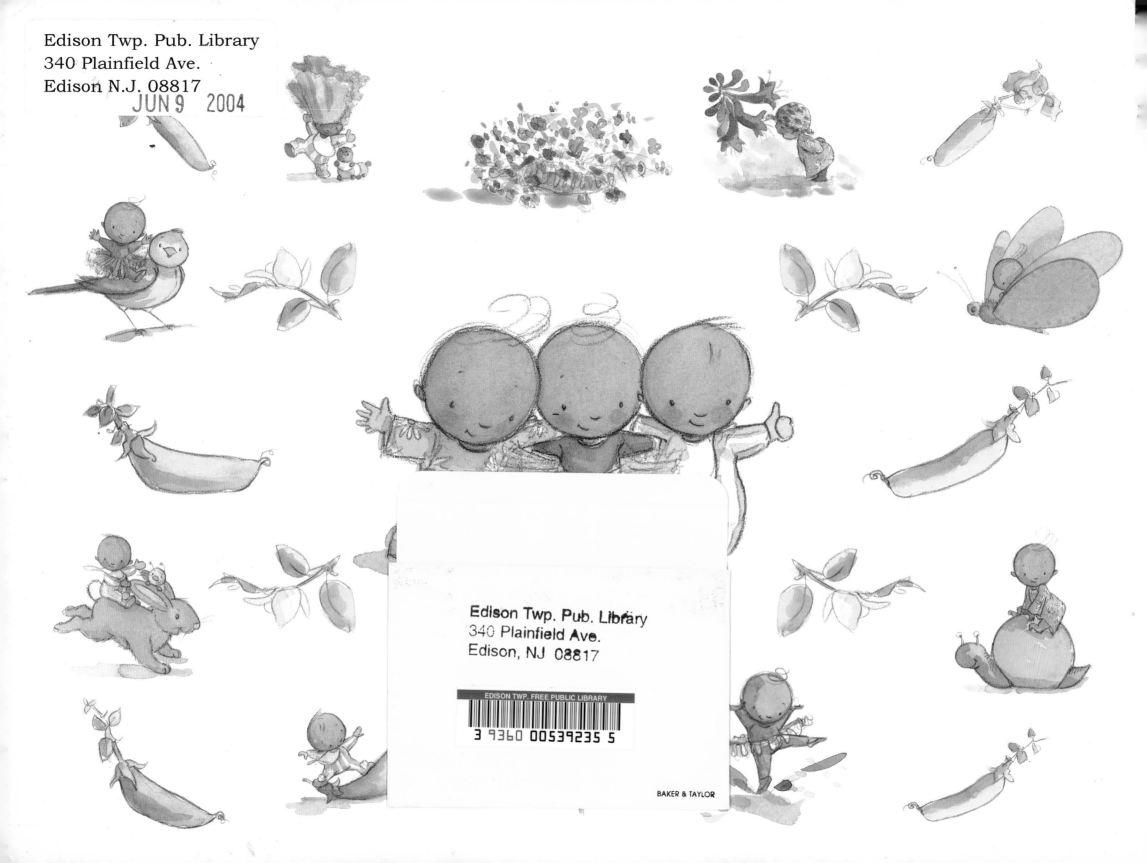